How to use the book ?

~ *Color the pages*
~ *Frame the colored pages*

OR

~ *Take a picture*
~ *Print on mugs, T-Shirts*
~ *Enjoy the cool graphics*

OR

~ *Use the graphics for tattoos*
~ *Use the graphics for Hena*

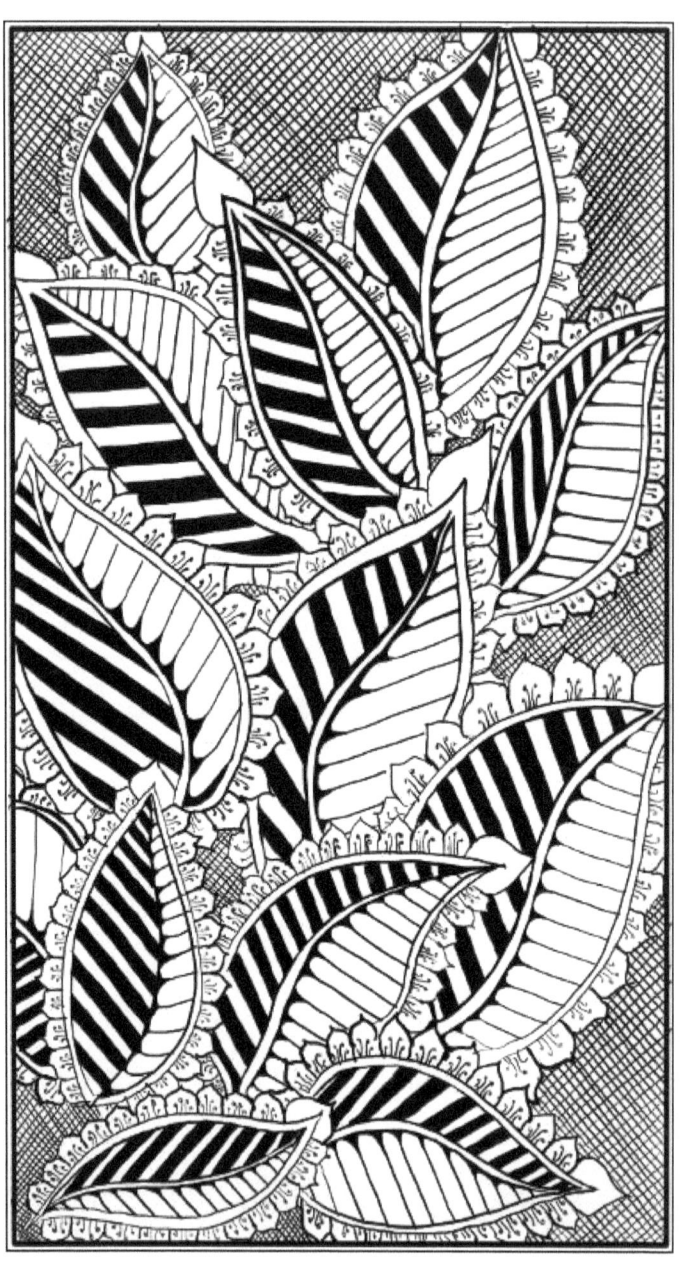

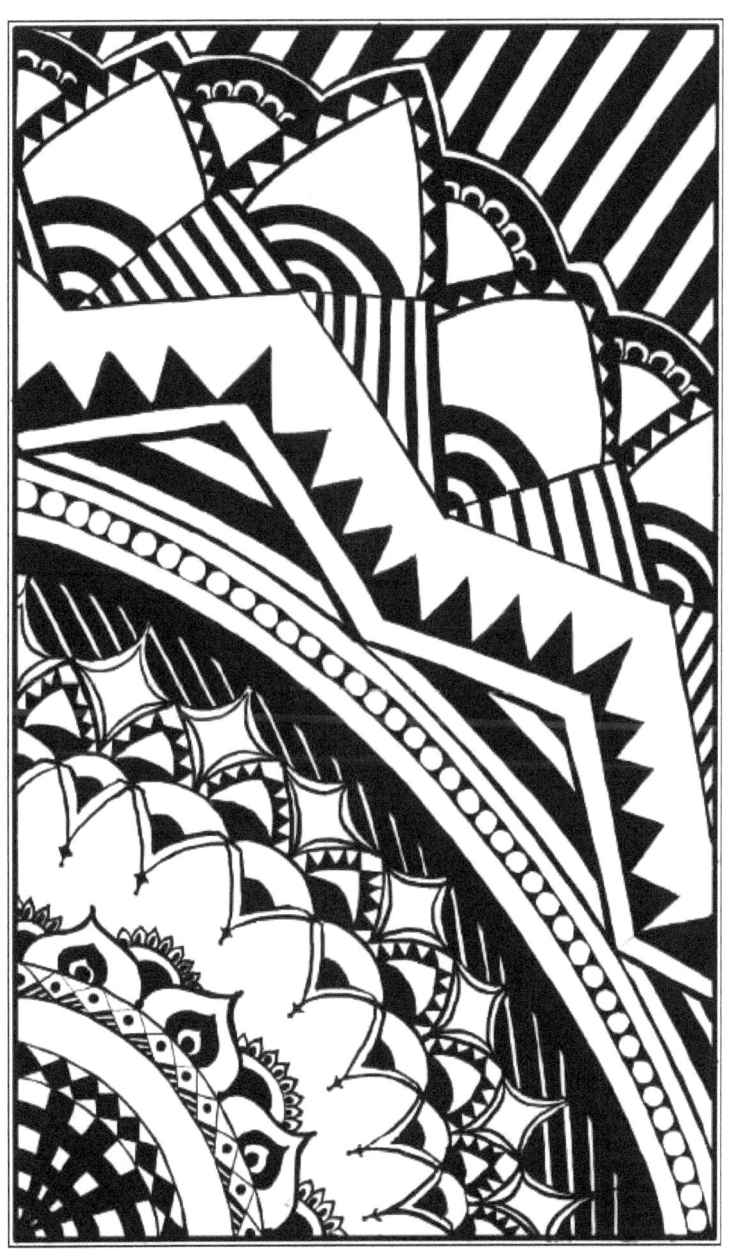

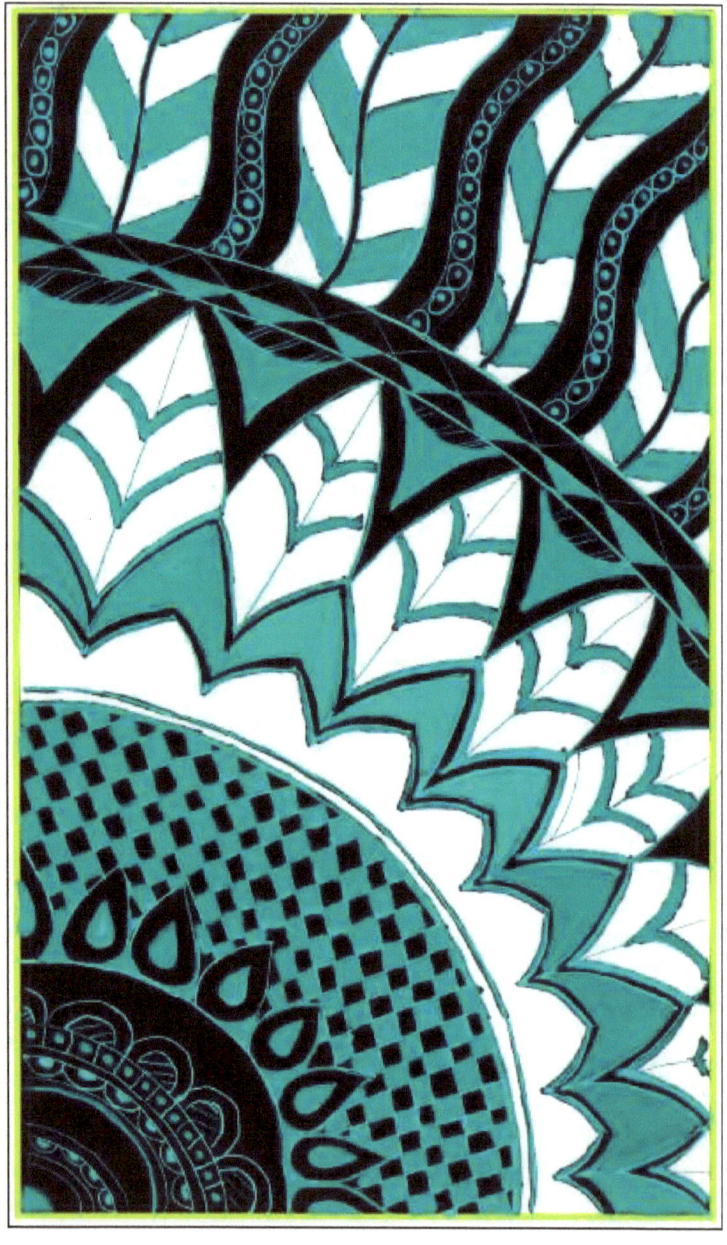

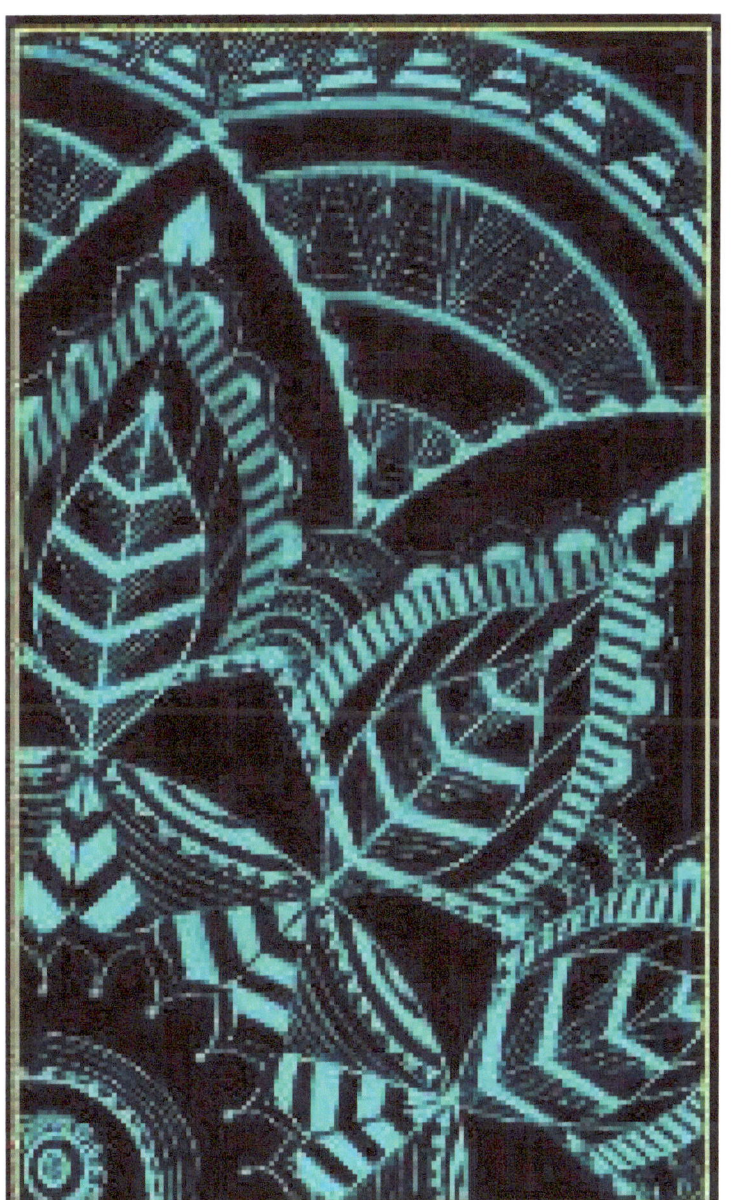

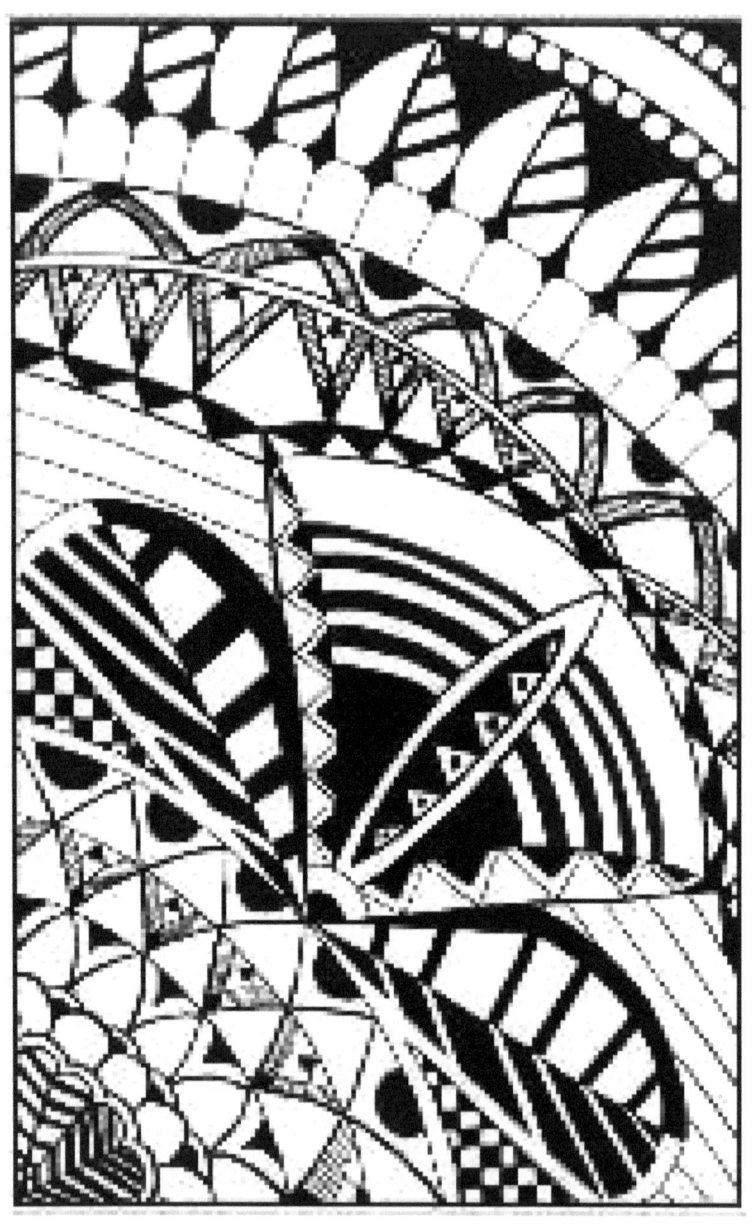

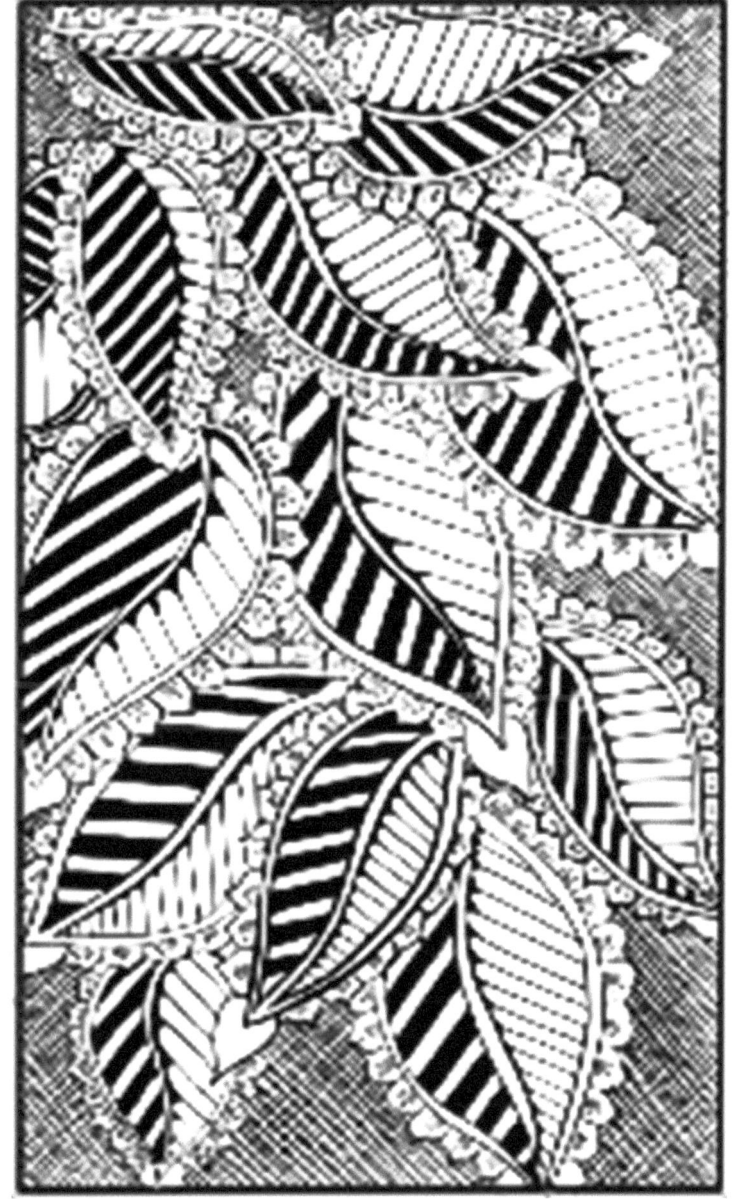

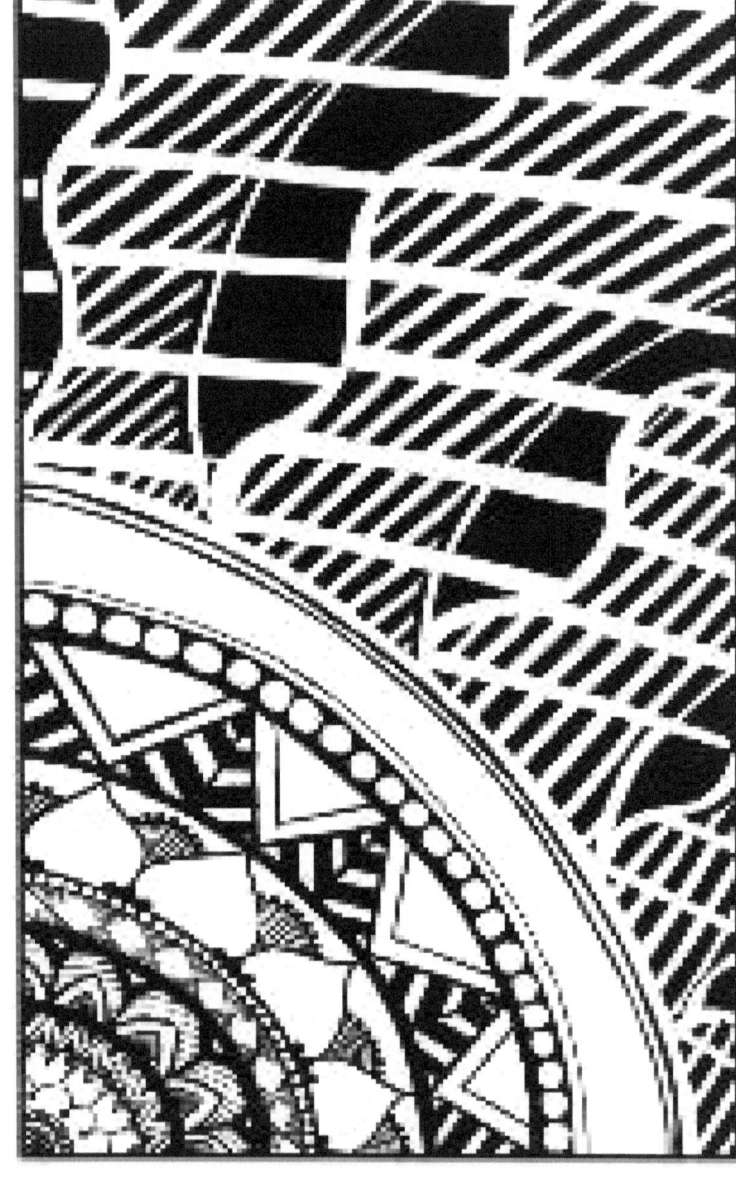

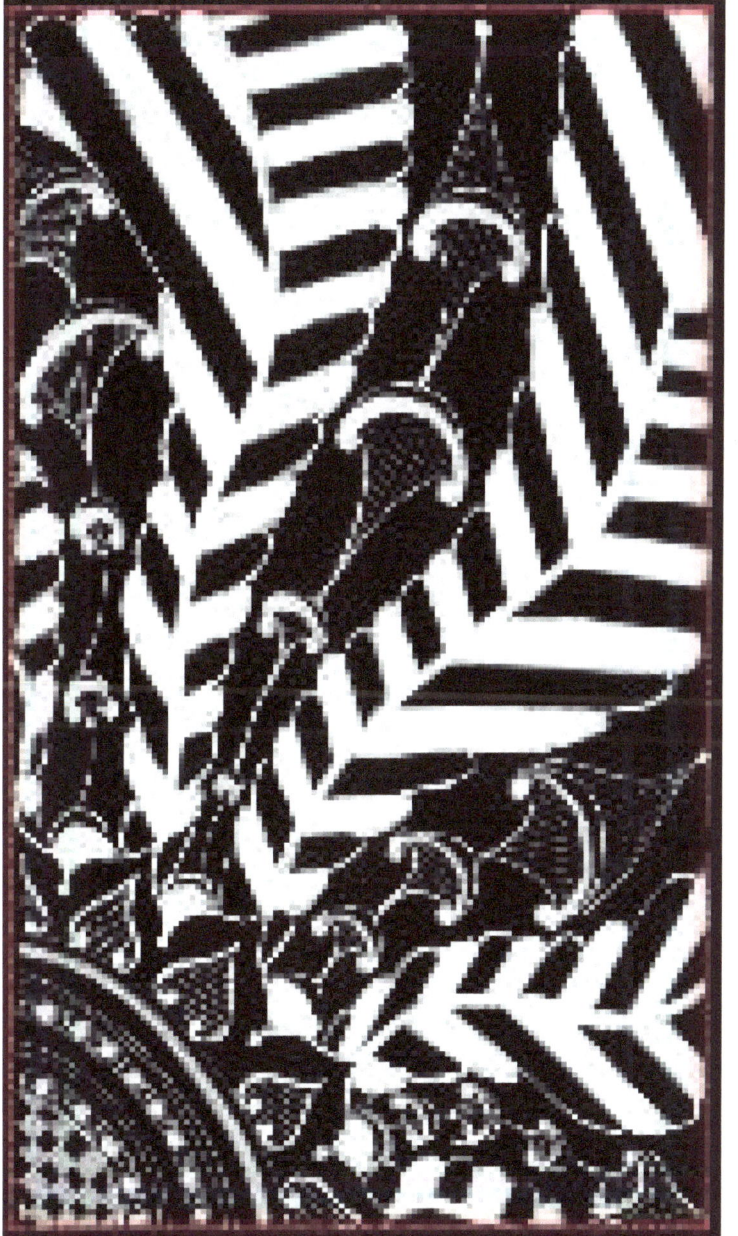

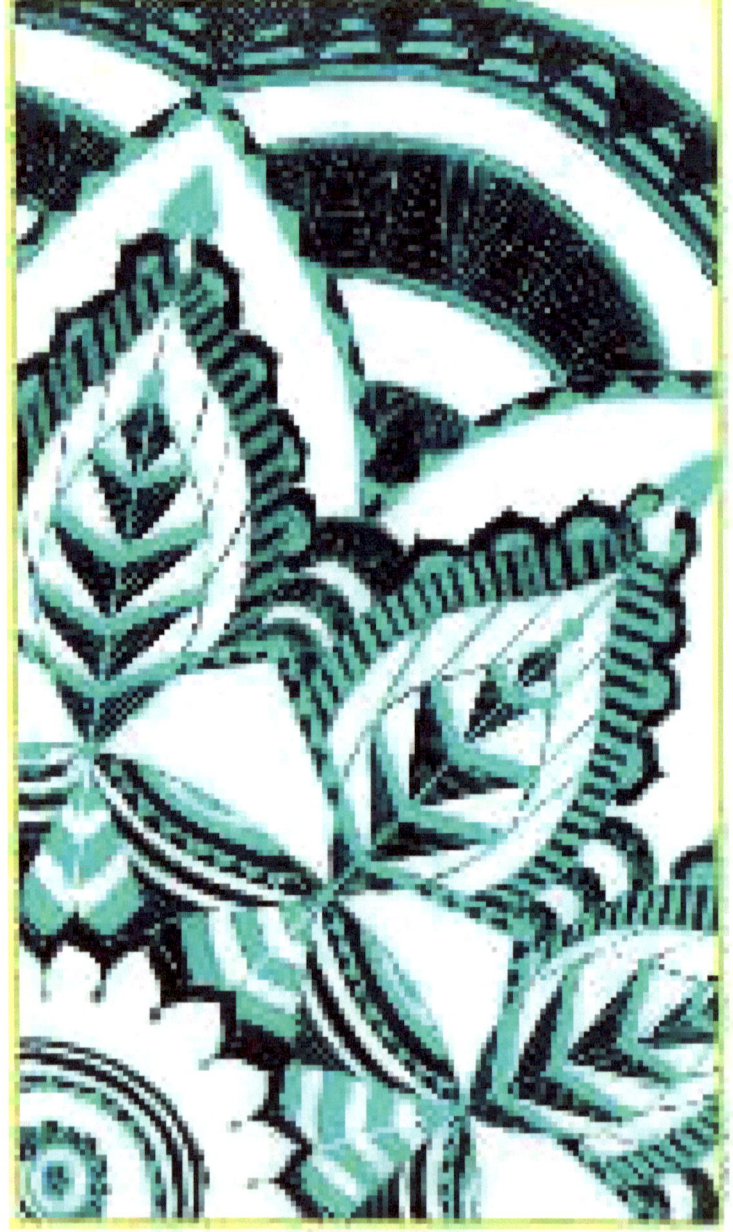

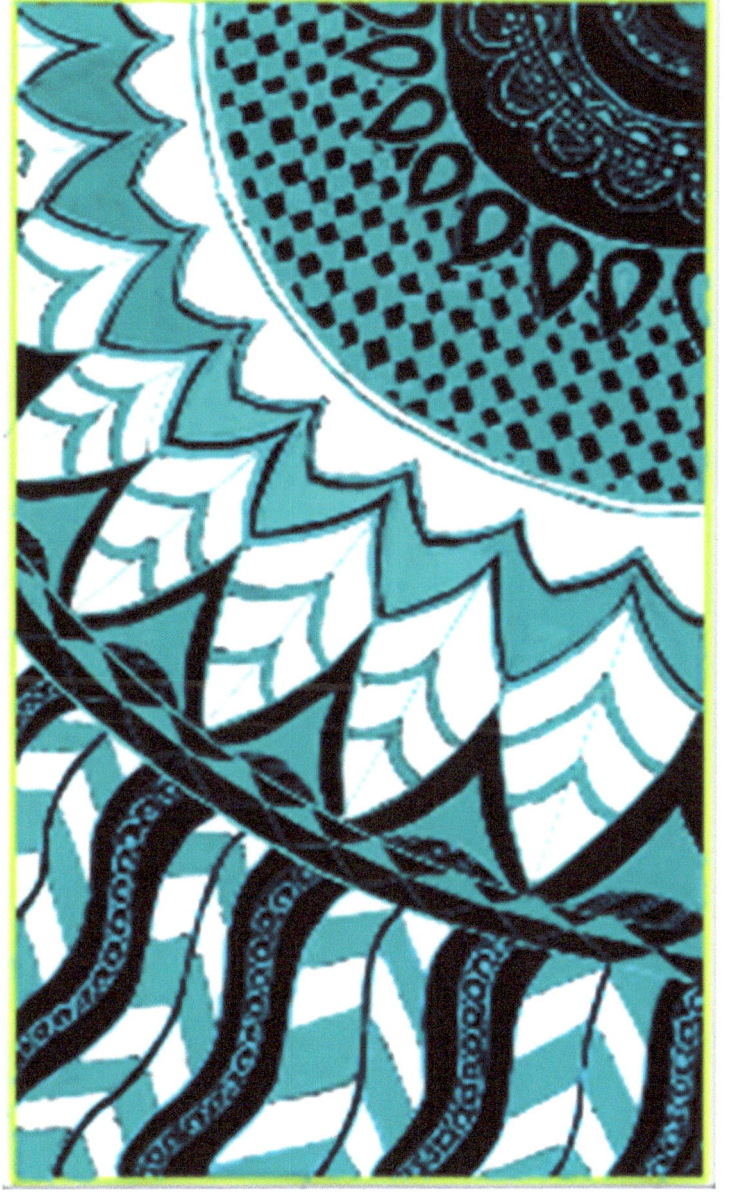

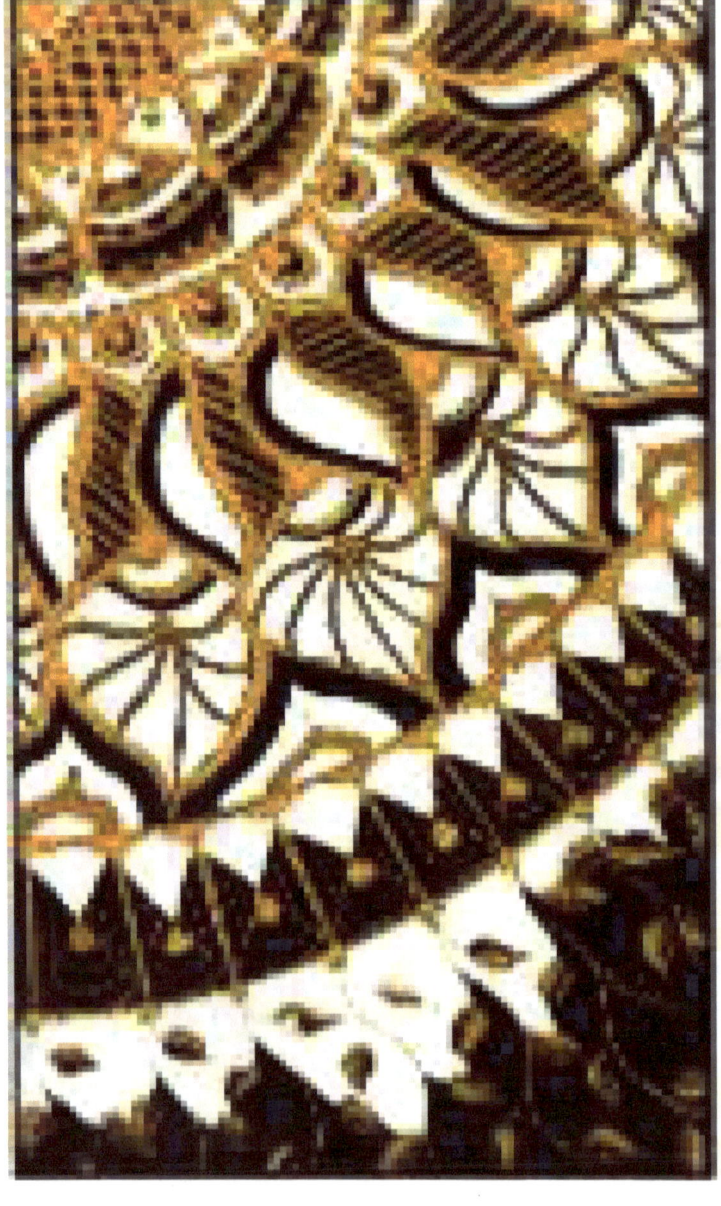

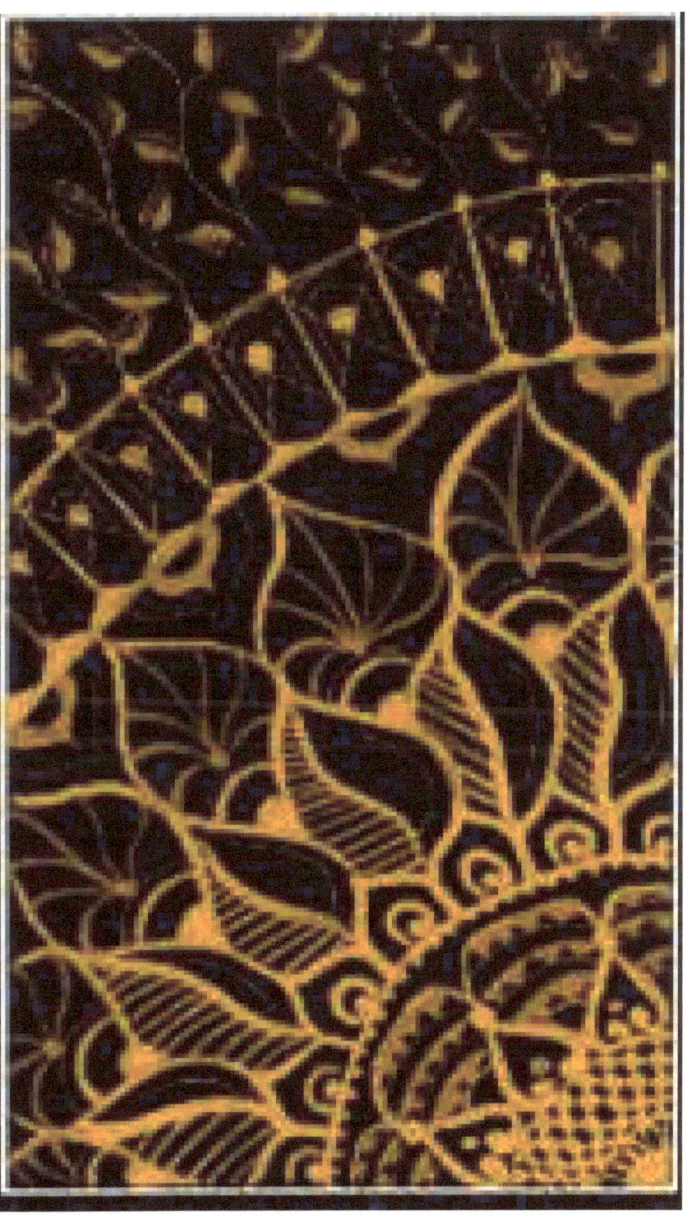

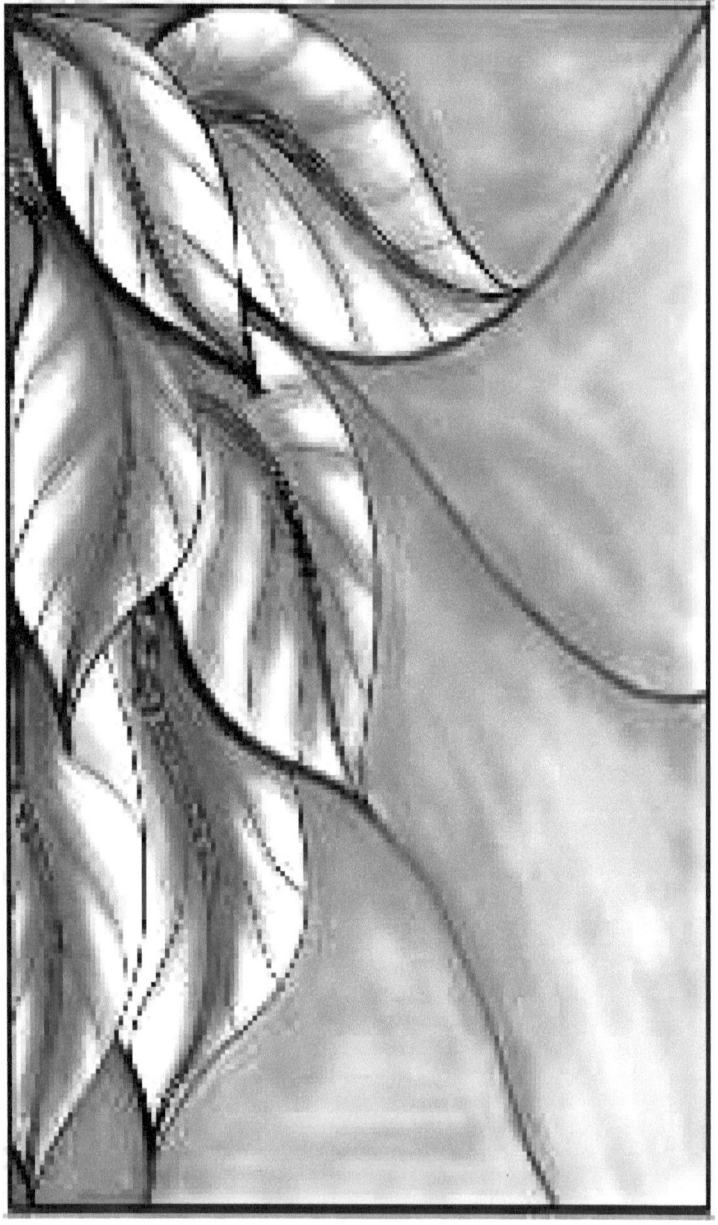

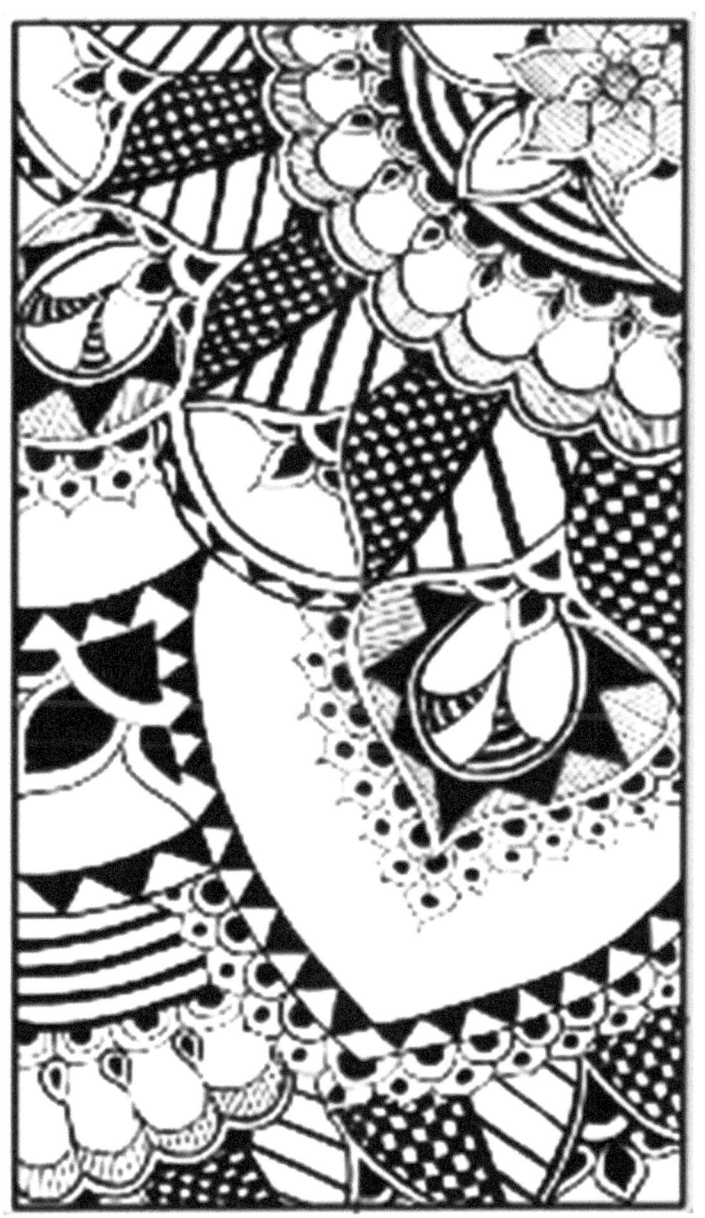

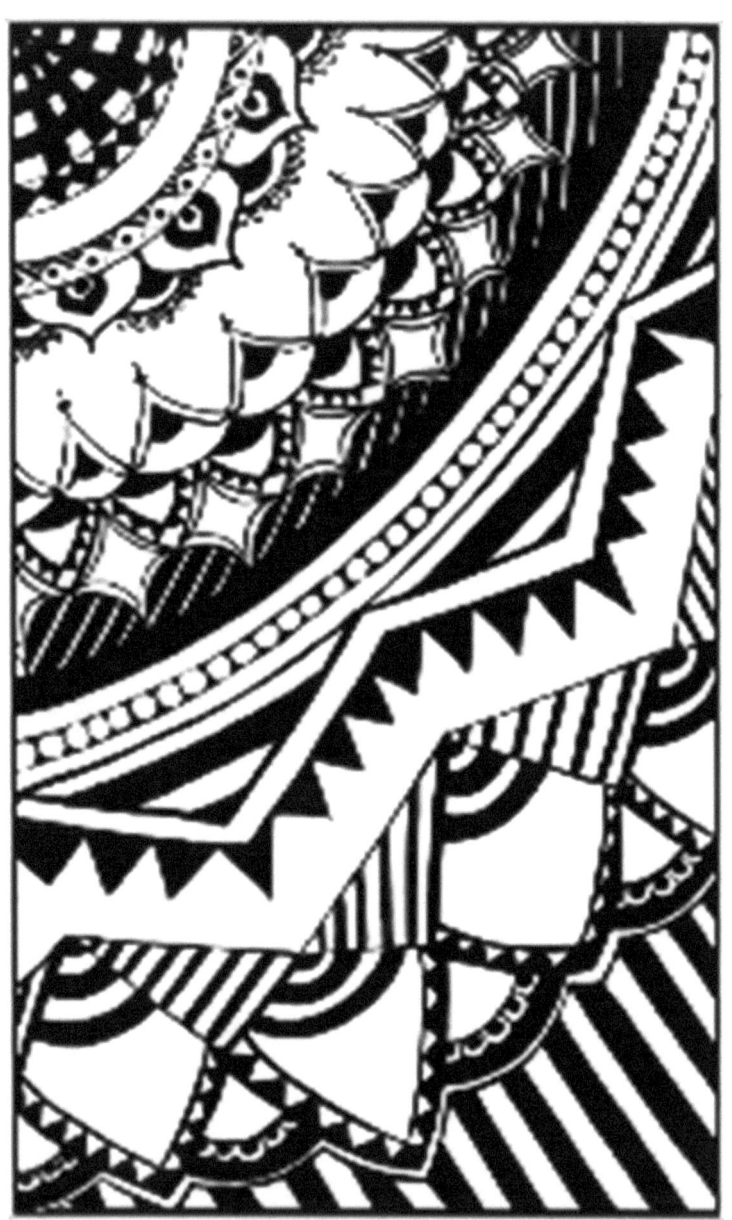

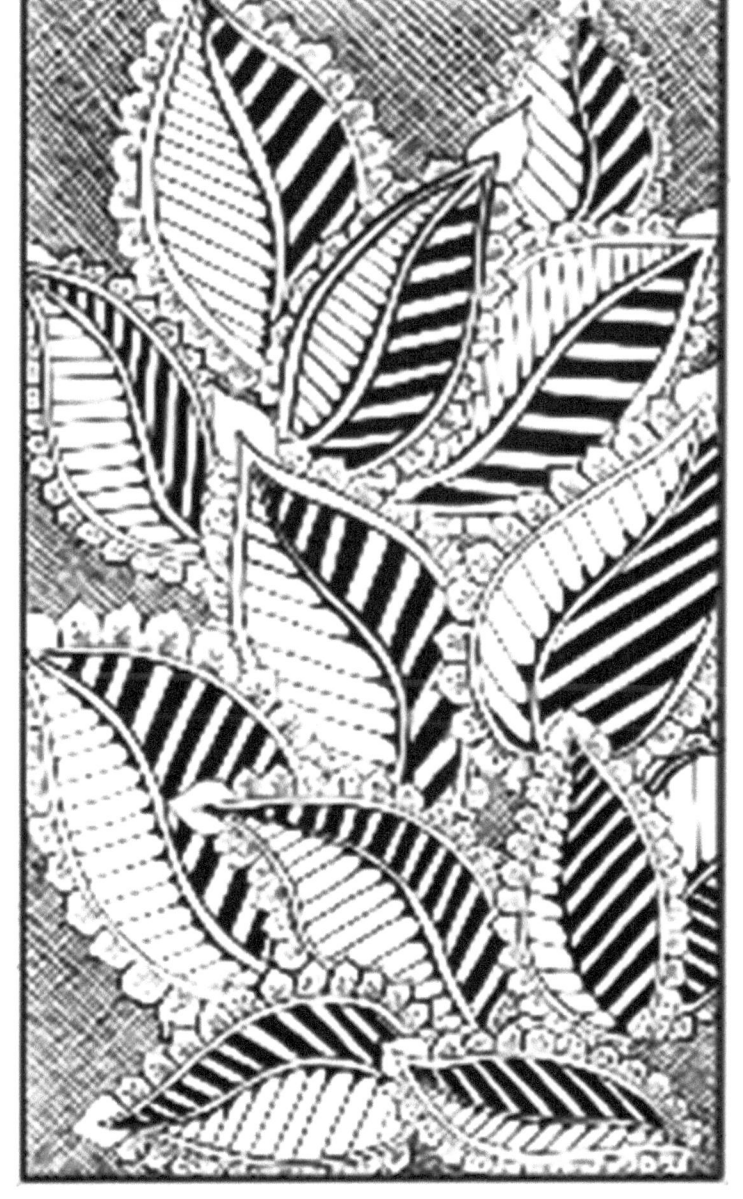

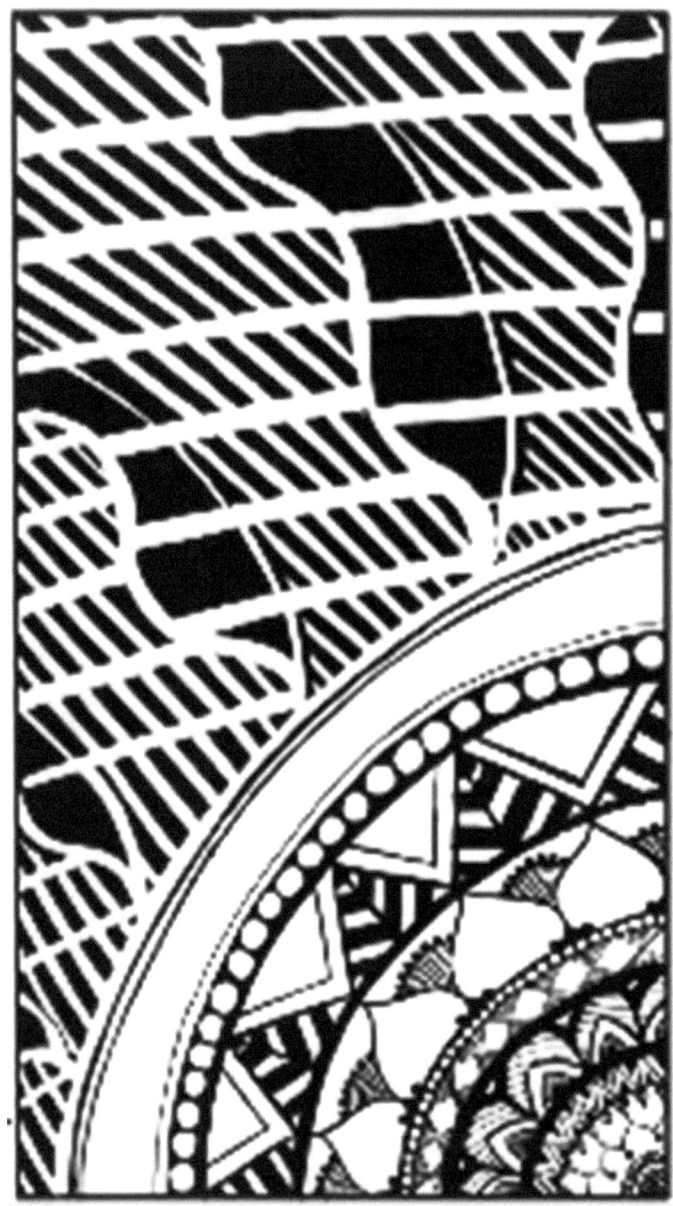

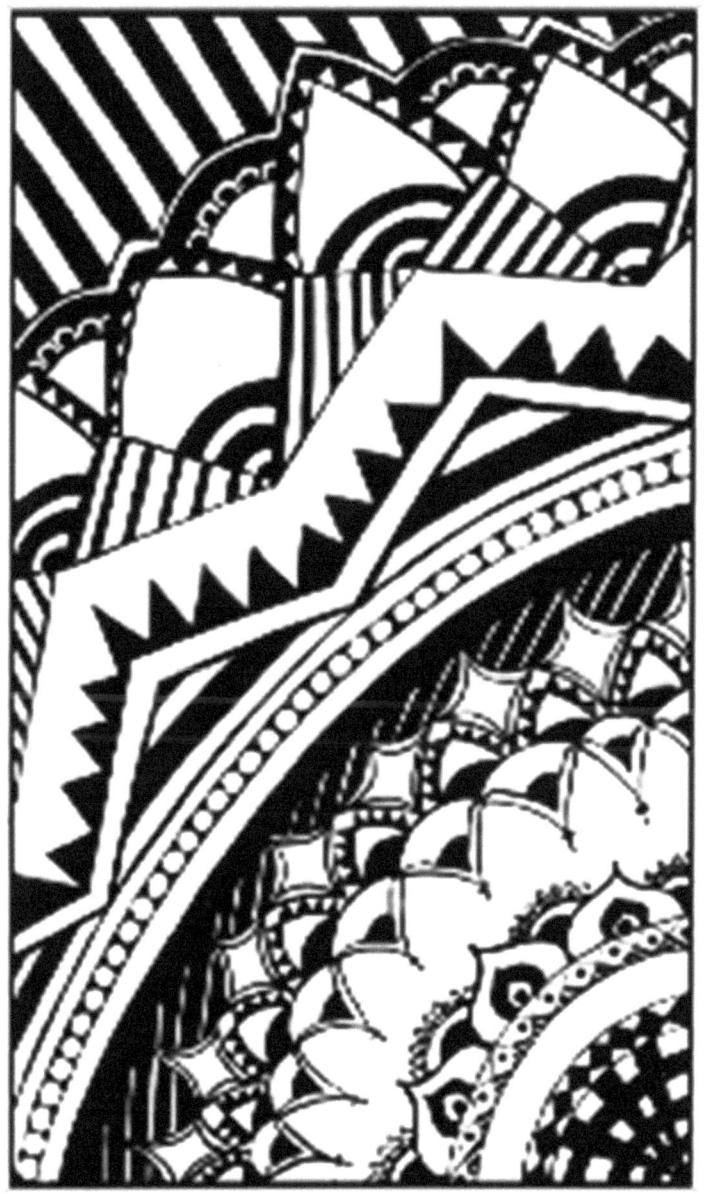

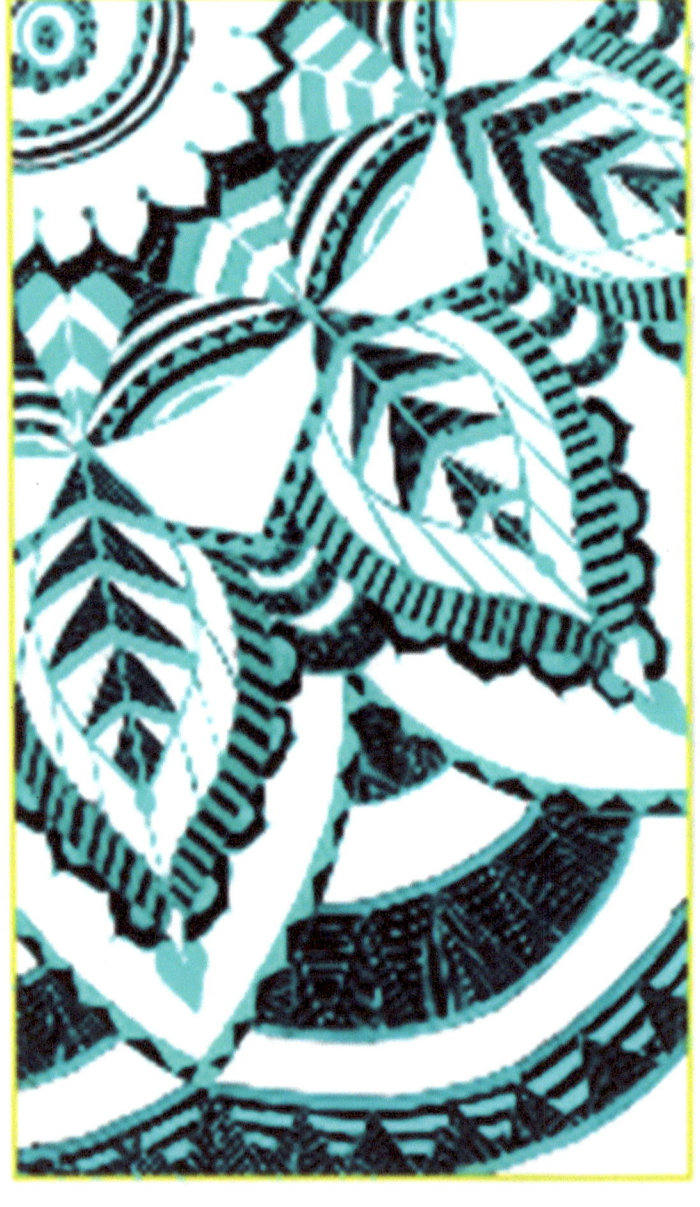

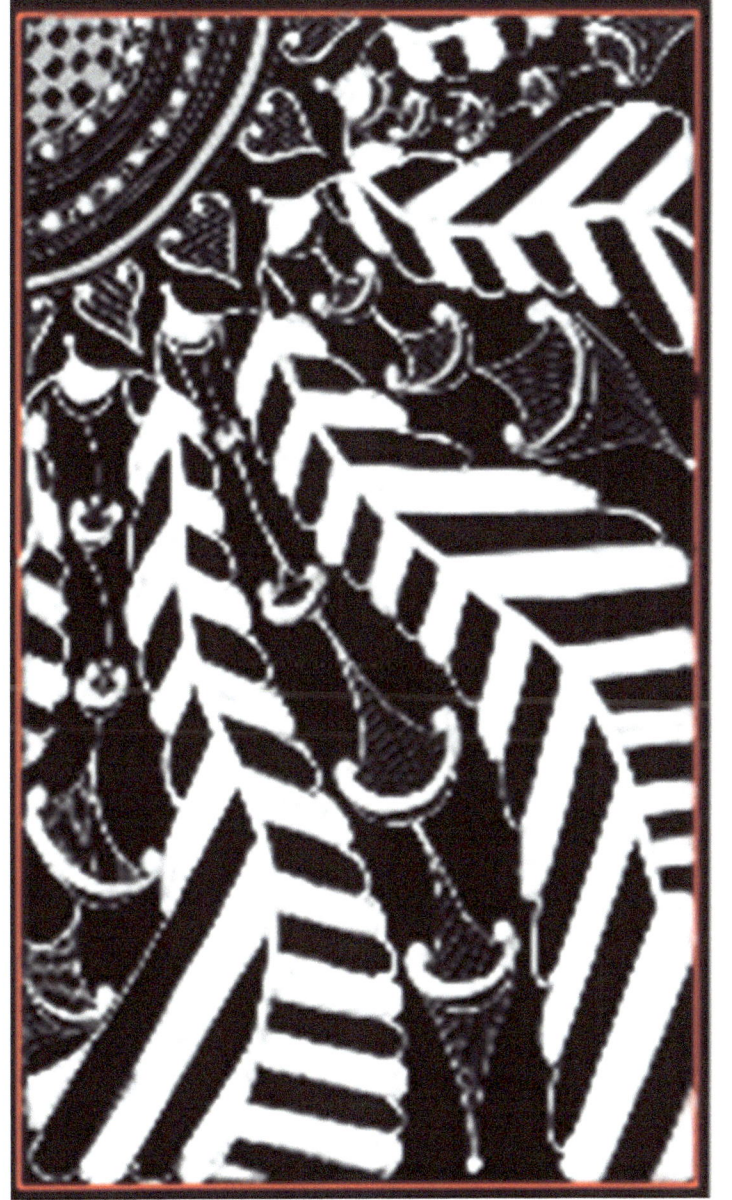

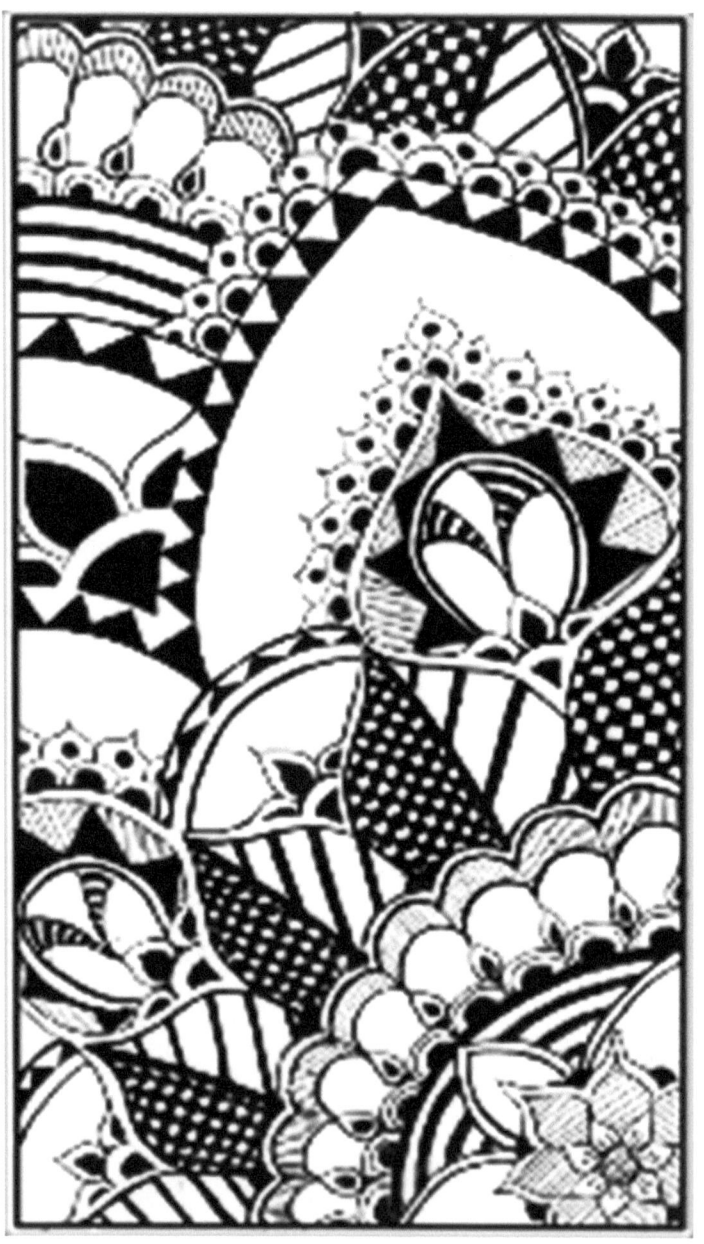

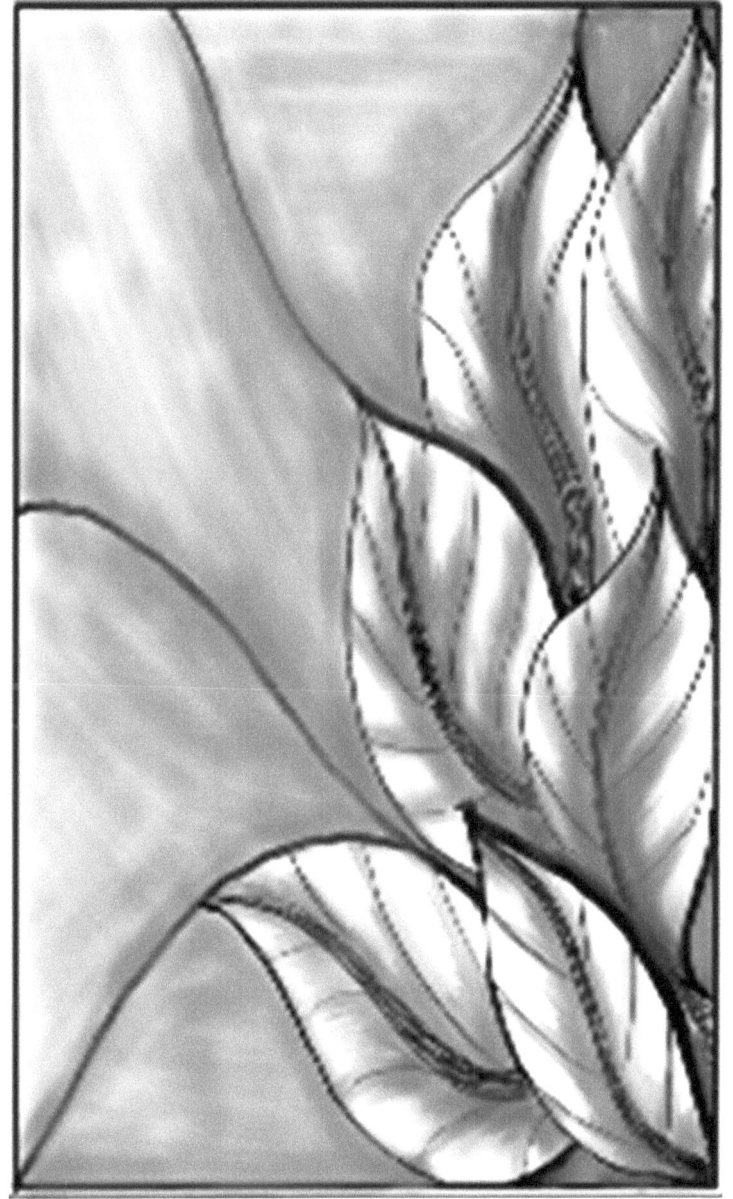

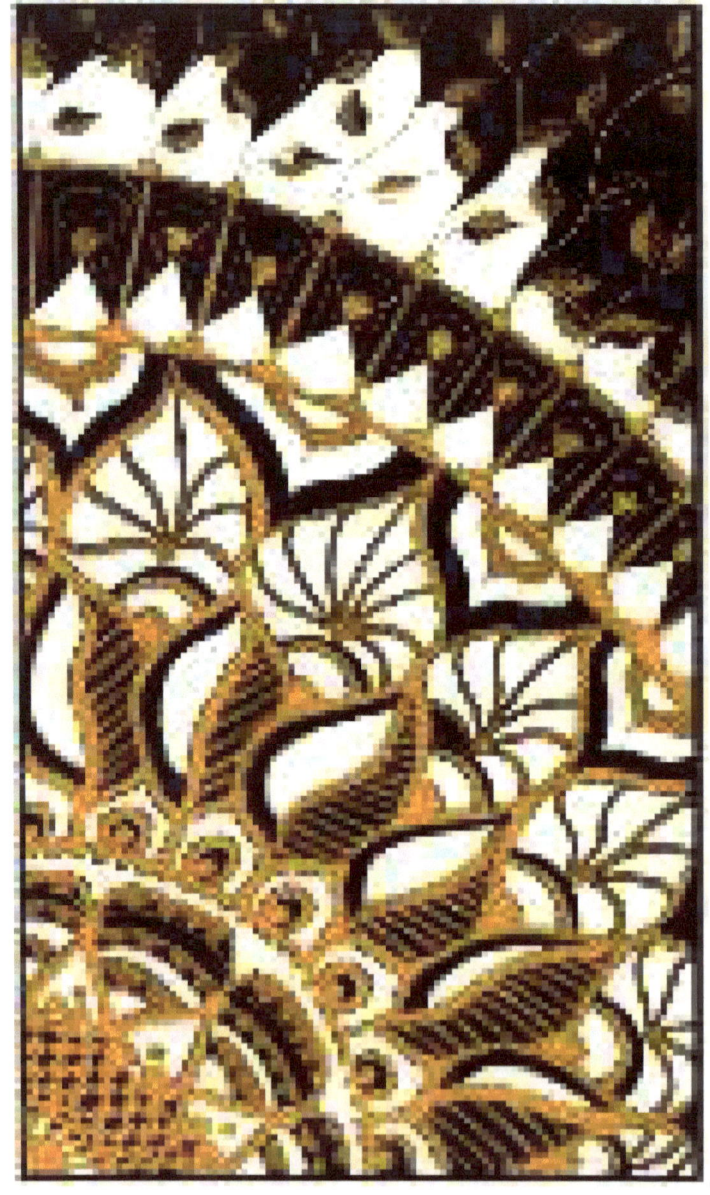

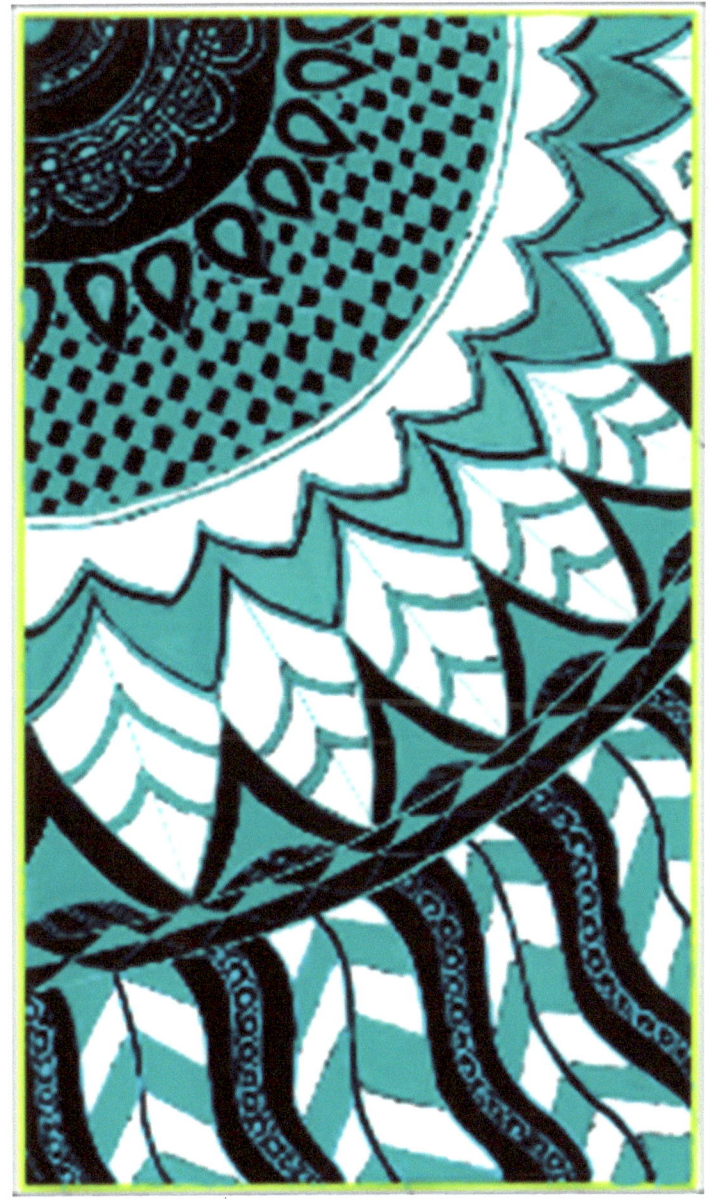

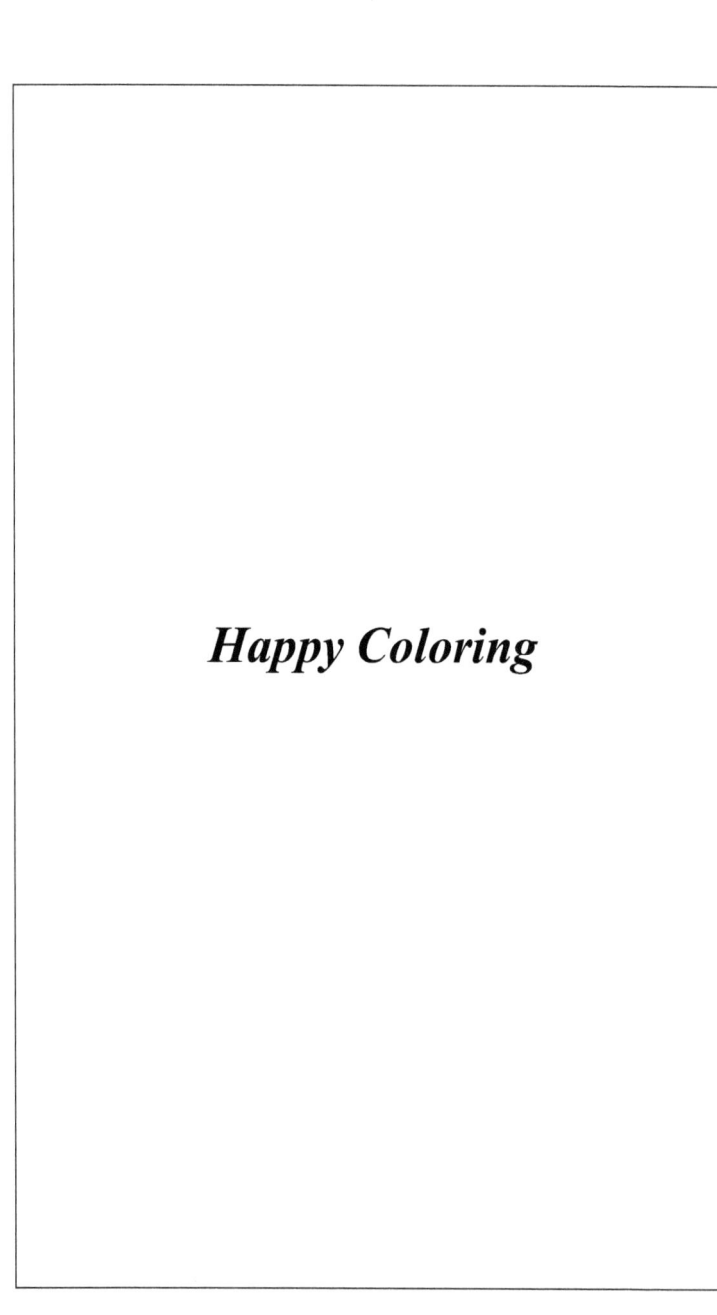
Happy Coloring

www.ingramcontent.com/pod-product-compliance
Lightning Source LLC
Chambersburg PA
CBHW040349220526
45473CB00009B/2820